FOLLOWING GOD

INTO THE CAGE

A 40-Day Devotional Journey

Alisa Hope Wagner

Scriptures taken from multiple translations of the Bible.

Author and cover photo by "sPidA" Garay

ISBN-13: 978-0692360798 (Custom Universal)
ISBN-10: 0692360794
BISAC: Religion / Christian Life / Devotional

FOLLOWING GOD

INTO THE CAGE

A 40-day Devotional

INTRODUCTION

If there were ever a boot camp for life, filming a reality television show would qualify. I found myself in the middle a reality TV show after our pastor mentioned that one would be holding tryouts at our church. I was transformed from a "writer" into a "MMA fighter," and I learned a lot about who I was in Christ during those two grueling months of training and filming.

I wrote a 40-day devotional about *following God into the cage*. I literally had to *follow* Him in obedience because there were many times I just wanted to run away. The dynamic of learning something new and having it filmed was interesting to say the least. I forced my faith to grow in a crazy situation that was unfamiliar and uncomfortable to me. But my faith did grow, and my relationship with God was transformed in the process!

Join me on my journey. I promise you won't have to "eat" punches, rush to the ER or spend sixty minutes in a sauna, but I think your faith will stretch along with mine. There's something supernatural about hearing the "word of their testimony" in Christ. We are strengthened to confront the challenges that God has placed before us when we see others face difficulty and find victory.

I believe that if I can walk into a cage fight, you can overcome any obstacle that stands in your way. Just give God your obedience, and He will give you His victory.

"They triumphed over him by the blood of the Lamb and by the **word of their testimony**; they did not love their lives so much as to shrink from death" (Revelations 12.11 NIV) (emphasis added).

* Watch the __Following God into the Cage Book Trailer__ at Alisa Hope Wagner's YouTube Channel along with her other videos.

Other books in the series: __Following God onto the Stage__ and __Following God across the Page__.

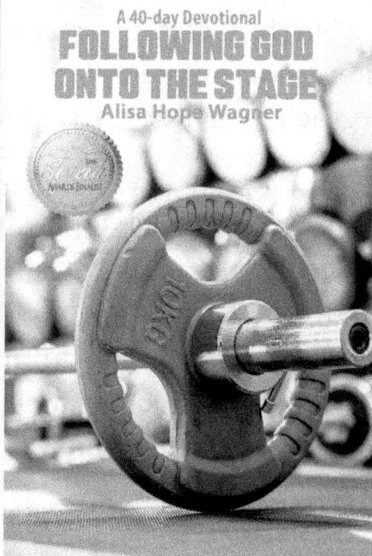

DEDICATION

God, my Creator, my Savior, my Counselor

Daniel, my high school sweetheart and soul mate

Isaac, my firstborn son

Levi, my brown-eyed boy

Karis Ruth, my cherished girl

Christina, my twin and friend.

Thank you to Patti Coughlin and Faith Newton for your edits and to "sPidA" Garay for the author and cover photos.

TABLE OF CONTENTS

DAY 1: WHEAT AND WEEDS

"When the crop began to grow and produce grain, the weeds also grew" (Matthew 13.26 NLT).

When I watched my reality TV show for the first time, I was so embarrassed. The fact is that I'm not perfect, and several of my flaws were on display. I fumed over my obvious mistakes and even called several of the producers. I said some things out of my insecurity, and I begged them to change some scenes or at least let me give explanations. Of course, nothing can be done once a project is finalized, so I cried out to God. Why would He lead me into a direction just to showcase my weakness? Was I so far gone that He needed to humble me in front of everyone?

Finally, God got my attention with one question: "What is more powerful? Your mistakes or my grace?" I realized that I had been committing idolatry. I put more emphasis on my mistakes than on God's sovereign authority. We are all sinners, and everything we create for God will have flaws, but those flaws will not stop God from establishing His glory. In fact, God can easily display His power in our weakness.

Jesus used the parable of the wheat and the weeds to illustrate that we will always find some things that we don't like about a person, a ministry, a job, a book, a school, a family, etc. However, that doesn't mean we should discredit all the wheat (virtue) because of a few weeds (flaws). When God gave me this truth, I fell in love with my show. I can see God's glory all over it, and my little mistakes now seem so insignificant.

"But he said to me, 'My grace is sufficient for you, for my power is made perfect in weakness.' Therefore I will boast all the more gladly about my weaknesses, so that Christ's power may rest on me" (2 Corinthians 12.9 NIV).

God, help me to realize that my mistakes are no match for your grace. I will never be perfect, but my flaws will not hinder me from walking out on faith for You. I'm determined not to judge others by their weaknesses; instead, I want to focus on the harvest of goodness that You are growing in them. I know that when I keep my eyes on You, the glory produced will outweigh all of my mess-ups. I pray this in Jesus' name, Amen.

Questions

1) Have you ever harvested something beautiful for the Lord only to realize there were a few weeds in your crop?

2) Does knowing that no person or ministry will be perfect help you to offer mercy and grace more freely?

3) By faith, will you recognize that Jesus makes all of our works pleasing to God when they are done in obedience?

Don't let the weeds stop you from growing the wheat!

DAY 2: ENCOURAGE YOURSELF

"David was greatly distressed, for the men spoke of stoning him because the souls of them all were bitterly grieved, each man for his sons and daughters. But David encouraged and strengthened himself in the Lord his God" (1 Samuel 30.6 AMP).

When I trained for Mix Martial Arts, I had several trainers pour their hearts and talents into me. Having multiple teachers helped me to learn fast, but that quick growth came at a high cost. I had major growing pains for two months. I was overwhelmed, exhausted and changing physically, mentally, emotionally and spiritually every single day! Not only is MMA Cage Fighting one of the hardest sports in existence, it was also completely foreign to me. I was starting from ground zero, trying to get into fighting condition in eight weeks.

At nights I wouldn't take any Aspirin because I had to take them to get through my two daily training sessions. I would lie awake in bed with a heating pad on my neck (where I pulled all my muscles) and an ice pack on my chest (where I had chest contusions), and I would cry out in pain because everything hurt. I could barely move, and I still had dozens of training and sparring sessions left to go. All I could do during those long nights was encourage myself in the Lord.

I'd tell myself over and over again that God had a plan for this craziness, and that it would all be over soon. I'd remind myself that God would not allow me to go through anything that He did not think I could handle. Trusting that God had a purpose for my pain made it easier to bear, and I firmly believed that He would use it to shine His glory. I found strength in God when I reached my limit, and I forced myself to stretch beyond my current capacity. As I look back, those nights are now some of my sweetest memories. I clung tightly to God, and He helped me to push through and reach my victory.

"No, in all these things we are more than conquerors through him who loved us" (Romans 8.37 NIV).

God, thank You for getting me through those difficult nights and bringing me closer into relationship with You. I praise You for teaching me how to encourage and strengthen myself in You. God, You helped me accomplish the challenge that You set before me, and my faith in You has grown stronger and deeper. I pray this in Jesus' name, Amen.

Questions

1) Have you ever had to encourage yourself in the promises that God has given you?

2) Do you rely too much on the words of affirmation from others and less on the truth God has given you?

3) Will you learn the discipline of finding encouragement in God alone, especially when you feel defeated?

Claim the victory that God has for you today!

DAY 3: SACRED INTIMACY

"When the priests enter them, they shall not go out of the holy *chamber* into the outer court; but there they shall leave their garments in which they minister, for they *are* holy. They shall put on other garments; then they may approach *that* which *is* for the people" (Ezekiel 42.14 NKJV).

I talk about God a lot; and when I was filming the reality TV show, He was apparent in my thoughts, actions and words. I find satisfaction in mulling over His character, His movements and His Word, and I can't help but mention everything He's showing me. Yes, the trainers and producers thought I was a little weird, but I enjoyed discussing my spirituality.

I say this because when I saw the show for the first time, I noticed that only a few of my God-nods made it into the final cut. (And to be honest, a ton of stuff had to be cut because there just wasn't enough space). At first I felt guilty, and I worried that the audience wouldn't see enough of God in my life; but God really reaffirmed me in His Word. I read that the priests needed to change out of the clothes they wore to minister (serve) God in the Holy Sanctuary before they entered into the courtyard where the people were.

We all have our Holy place with God, and our intimacy might confuse, disturb or even hurt others. Non-Christians may think we're complete lunatics if they don't know us personally, and other Christians may feel like they need to force their intimacy with God to resemble ours.

When Jesus revealed His perfect intimacy with God in His transfiguration, He was only around His three closest friends (Mark 9.2). I shouldn't feel like I need to reveal the intimate aspects of my relationship with Christ to the masses. I must trust that my walk of faith will bear evidence of my close relationship with Him, and that the life I lead will cause people to notice a difference. Once people see my strength in Christ, I can be ready for when the Holy Spirit opens the door for me to offer a glimpse of my own transformation into His image.

> "So all of us who have had that veil removed can see and reflect the glory of the Lord. And the Lord— who is the Spirit—makes us more and more like him as we are changed into his glorious image" (2 Corinthians 3.18 NLT).

God, I don't want to pile on guilt about not revealing enough of You. You have my heart, and I'm relieved to know that the bulk of my intimacy with You is special and private. I know that You are totally capable of establishing Your own glory, and I'm honored that You desire a personal, intimate relationship with me. I pray this in Jesus' name, Amen.

Questions

1) Does our intimacy with the Lord confuse people who are close to you?

2) How can you share some of your intimacy with God without making others feel uncomfortable or inferior?

3) Tell of a time that the Holy Spirit lead you to share a personal story about how God showed His love and care in your life.

Your relationship with Jesus will overflow onto others!

DAY 4: BROKEN-DOWN POTENTIAL

"Come, let us return to the Lord. He has torn us to pieces; now he will heal us. He has injured us; now he will bandage our wounds. In just a short time he will restore us, so that we may live in his presence" (Hosea 6.1-2 NLT).

When I trained for my MMA fight, I sparred with several different women. Sparring is extremely important because it prepares you for the cage. However, sparring hurts. One woman I sparred threw me against the cage, forcing her shoulder – and all of her body weight – into my chest. I felt my sternum crunch, so I took a visit to the E.R. Another woman hit my nose, causing it to swell and bruise, and every additional punch to my face felt like a hammer. And another woman put me into so many arm bars that I thought my arm would fall off.

After each injury, my sparring partners would give me a hug and say, "Good job." They didn't feel guilty about the pain they inflicted on me because they knew that they were helping me find my victory. Sounds strange, doesn't it? But they were breaking me down, so I could become stronger. By the time I entered the cage, my injuries were healed (for the most part), and I was strong. After a minute and nine seconds, I won my fight by TKO (Technical Knock Out). I gave my opponent a hug, and said, "God will break you down, but I promise He will build you back up again."

God needs to unleash the amazing potential in each of us, and He can only do it when we are broken and surrendered to Him. Sometimes God will use situations to break us, but other times He will use people. I used to struggle when God wanted to use me as a tool to break someone down, but now I am filled with the understanding that if their hearts are open to Him, He will build them back up even stronger and wiser than before.

Although I'm not going to actively seek out being God's breaking instrument, I won't shy away from it either. I want all of God's children to reach their potential in Christ, and I know that He is fully capable of healing and strengthening those whose eyes are focused on Him.

> "Therefore encourage one another and build each other up, just as in fact you are doing" (1 Thessalonians 5.11 NIV).

God, please help me not be offended when others are used to break me. Whether they are aware of it or not, they are a tool to build my faith and bring me closer to You. Also, help me to be used to sharpen others with confidence and grace. I care more about them becoming like You than about them having comfortable, painless lives. I pray this in Jesus' name, Amen.

Questions

1) Do you have trouble humbling yourself to others?

2) Did you know that God may use people to shape and mold you?

3) Can you think of a time that someone tried to break you, but God used that experience to make you stronger in Him?

God will tear you down to make you stronger!

DAY 5: HOPE DEFERRED

"Hope deferred makes the heart sick, but a longing fulfilled is a tree of life" (Proverbs 13.12 NIV).

One of my MMA trainers asked me what my favorite verse was. She wanted to have the verse printed on my fight shirt. I instantly thought of my favorite Proverbs verse, which has been my heart's cry for many years. I didn't think the verse fit the whole MMA vibe, but I felt the Holy Spirit prompting me to choose it. A couple of hours before my fight, my trainer and her designer handed me my personally designed shirt that boasted a hand-drawn image of my MMA gloved hand holding a pen.

How fitting—the fighter and the writer! As I began my journey of becoming a writer many years ago, I found that God consistently called me into what I thought were failures. I would pour my heart, strength and energy into every task He placed in front of me. I would sacrifice my free time, force myself to grow and learn, and continually seek His guidance. My string of dead-ends confused me. I'd put forth the hard work only to come up empty handed every time. However, when my spirit soaked up Proverbs 13.12, I finally found understanding.

Jesus is the Tree of Life, and when we fully embrace Him, our lives will be filled with the outpouring of His glory. Instead of simply grabbing hold of a single fruit (blessing), I became determined to cling onto the entire Tree. Only in Jesus will I ever find complete peace, complete joy, complete purpose, complete acceptance and complete life! All the other fruits on the tree are products of Jesus' awesomeness, and they manifest themselves in different ways on this earth and in our lives. I trust that every time my hope is deferred, the hard work I put in will be reinvested into the Tree of Life. And when I'm finally able to pluck a few fruits from my Tree, they will be huge, juicy and ripe!

"Blessed are those who wash their robes, so that they may have the right to the tree of life and that they may enter the city by the gates" (Revelation 22.14 ESV).

God, help me to understand that blessings are merely the effects of who You are. Instead of wasting my energy reaching for a single blessing, show me how to live in Your presence so that Your blessings surround me. I have faith that every time I invest in the Tree of Life and my hope is deferred that my harvest of blessings is growing bigger because Your presence is growing stronger. I pray this in Jesus' name, Amen.

Questions

1) Have you tried satisfying your heart's desire with something other than Jesus, the Tree of Life, only to realize that the joy didn't last?

2) Do you know that every blessing is produced by allowing Jesus to become bigger and stronger in your life?

3) Have you tried to share the Tree of Life with others, so they too can have the ultimate gift of salvation?

Jesus is your complete joy!

DAY 6: POWER OF OBEDIENCE

"Do you not know that when you present yourselves to someone *as* slaves for obedience, you are slaves of the one whom you obey, either of sin resulting in death, or of obedience resulting in righteousness?" (Romans 6.16 NASB).

The five hours I waited before my fight (it was 10th out of 11 fights), I wouldn't open myself to emotion. Fear had boxed me in, so I flat-lined my feelings and relied solely on faith. Right before the promoters played my fight song—which began my long walk to the cage—I quickly exposed my fear to God. I told Him that I was scared, and that I wanted to run away. I felt God ask me one question: "If I told you to walk into that cage and get crushed for me, would you do it?" *Yes,* I thought. "Then you have nothing to worry about," He answered.

And in that moment, I felt the amazing depth of obedience. I talked a lot about obedience while filming for the reality TV show, and I was told that I shouldn't use that word since people really don't understand it. However, the truth is that obedience is extremely important because it can lead to life or death. We all have a choice: We can obey ourselves and our own desires or we can obey God and His amazing plan.

I would be a fool not to give my allegiance in God. I am a creation; He is the Creator. I want to submit myself to God, so He can be the leading force of my life and take me places I could never dream of going on my own. Why would I want to be the master of my own soul when the God of the Universe loves me more than I love myself? God created my life, and He knows how to fill it with His best.

After I won my fight, I was able to tell almost 2,000 people about the goodness of my God from center stage of the arena. I would have never gotten that opportunity if I had been obedient to my own desire of running away. I don't understand everything that God does, but I trust that His ways come together to form His perfect plan for me.

> "The thief comes only to steal and kill and destroy; I have come that they may have life, and have it to the full" (John 10.10 NIV).

God, I know that it is very difficult to let go of the controls and give my life as a living sacrifice to You. But I also trust that my life will have more meaning and power when it is submitted to Your authority. I want my life to make a difference and have a purpose, and I have faith that You will shine Your glory in my life when I stay obedient to Your will. I pray this in Jesus' name, Amen.

Questions

1) Has God called you into a situation that made you want to run and hide?

2) What happened when you decided to stay obedient to His leading?

3) Do you trust that God will only lead you down paths of righteousness?

Trust God's plan and obey His lead!

DAY 7: PROCESS OF CHANGE

"Jesus grew in wisdom and in stature and in favor with God and all the people" (Luke 2.52 NLT).

When I first met my lead trainer, he asked me if I had ever punched anyone. I said no. Then he asked me if I had ever been punched. Again, I said no. I knew very little about MMA when I began training, except for the small portion I learned while taking kickboxing for a semester during my college years. I was ignorant, uncomfortable and in over my head; and I had eight weeks to get ready.

Thankfully, my trainers didn't expect me to learn everything in a day. My body, mind, emotions and spirit wouldn't have been able to adapt to the mass influx of information, skill, and change. Everyday of my training spurred me into monumental growth, and there would have been no way for me to adjust to the transformation all at once. Each training session stretched my capacity to a centimeter of my breaking point, and I had precious little time to prepare for my next challenge.

My MMA training taught me a lot about my spiritual growth. I've been very hard on myself through the years. Since I began my quest to live for Christ, I set ridiculous expectations and demanded immediate change. I had given myself no grace; and instead of taking each challenge as they came and allowing myself time to heal and strengthen, I expected constant perfection. However, I realized that I pushed the joy out of the process of development when I wouldn't give myself room to make mistakes and grow.

Life is filled with training sessions, and God doesn't expect us to know everything in one day. He gives us seasons of growth and rest, and joy is found when we walk in step with the Master

Trainer. Whenever I get discouraged about my spiritual transformation, I can rejoice in how much I've grown from the girl who knew absolutely nothing about a life of faith.

> "But grow in the grace and knowledge of our Lord and Savior Jesus Christ. To him be glory both now and forever! Amen" (2 Peter 3.18 NIV).

God, You see the end result of my life, and You see the potential of what I could be. I understand that my process of change won't happen in a day, but You will accomplish Your design throughout the combined days of my life. Help me to embrace grace as I daily grow in wisdom and stature. I pray this in Jesus' name, Amen.

Questions

1) Do you have trouble walking gracefully in your mistakes?

2) Did you know that God is fully able to work out His perfect plan even in your imperfection?

3) Can you embrace the good work that God is doing in your life every day without fretting over how you stumble along the way?

Don't let fear of failure prevent you from walking by faith!

DAY 8: SPIRITUAL STORMS

"He will sit like a refiner of silver, burning away the dross. He will purify the Levites, refining them like gold and silver, so that they may once again offer acceptable sacrifices to the Lord" (Malachi 3.3 NLT).

When I flew to Florida to train at a gym, a spiritual storm that tested my faith began to build. I was away from my family, in unfamiliar territory, with unfamiliar people and learning an unfamiliar sport. My trainers worked diligently to prepare me for my fight, and I obediently did everything they asked of me. However, inside anxiety took a hold of me, and the night before my final training day in Florida, I fell victim to fear.

Instead of kneeling on the floor of my hotel room, praying for God's guidance and peace, I turned off my phone and booked a flight home. I blamed everyone for my fear, and I justified my actions. A week later God confronted my mistakes, and I confessed my trail of actions spawned by my lack of faith. I was afraid, and I pointed my finger at everyone else but myself. Finally, God got a hold of me with one simple truth: *He had placed me there*. If I was going to blame anyone, I would have to blame Him.

God was putting me through a very humbling process that exposed the defenses I had built because I didn't trust Him. God allows us to go through storms when He knows we are strong enough to persevere. He puts us through the fire because He is trying to purify us and shape us into His image. I know that trials are never easy and spiritual storms are confusing, but now I'm prepared with the knowledge that God is growing me. Instead of running away from the next storm, I will dig in my heels, cling onto God and allow the flames to burn off my imperfections.

"These have come so that the proven genuineness of your faith—of greater worth than gold, which perishes even though refined by fire—may result in praise, glory and honor when Jesus Christ is revealed" (1 Peter 1.7 NIV).

God, I understand that You allow certain storms into my life. Although they each may appear different, they all are used to build my faith and shape me into Your image. Help me to trust You when I'm in the middle of the storm. Don't let me build up defenses that would prevent the fires from purifying me. I pray this in Jesus' name, Amen.

Questions

1) Have you experienced a crazy time in your life only to realize in retrospect that it was a spiritual storm?

2) Did you know that the best thing to do when under spiritual attack is to keep your eyes on Jesus and not the storm?

3) How can identifying the spiritual storms in your life better prepare you to hunker down and stay strong in faith?

Keep your eyes on Jesus to get through the storms of life!

DAY 9: SUPPORT OF MANY

"And let us consider how we may spur one another on toward love and good deeds, not giving up meeting together, as some are in the habit of doing, but encouraging one another—and all the more as you see the Day approaching" (Hebrews 10.24-25 NIV).

As the date of my fight got closer, I began to get more and more people involved. I would ask everyone to pray for me. I had two special pastors say prayers for me over the phone. My husband constantly had a *word* for me from His Bible reading. My twin sister fasted seven days for me. I arranged for several of my family and friends to attend my fight. My family sent me text messages of affirmation. My Facebook and Twitter friends posted their encouragement.

I told everyone who would listen about what God was doing in my life because I knew I couldn't do it on my own. I exposed my inability and my weakness, believing that I needed a movement of God's people to accomplish the task set before me. I know that I would have never persevered if it hadn't been for the support of many. I rallied others to accomplish God's will because I trusted His movement in my life. Our lives of faith will never achieve all that God has for us unless we are willing to receive help from others.

However, we must firmly believe in God's plan for our lives if we want people to come along side us. Our confidence in God's purpose must be obvious, and we need to trust that He works His perfect will in our imperfections. Standing boldly on His word and His call will encourage others to help us along the path to which God has called us.

"Dear friends, if our hearts do not condemn us, we have confidence before God (1 John 3.12 NIV).

God, I want to be willing to admit that I can't do it all by myself, and I understand that I'll only reach the goals that You set for me if I lean on others. Strengthen my faith in Your plan for my life, so that I can gather the support of many. I want to be a part of something bigger than myself, and I'm willing to humble myself to accomplish Your amazing will. I pray this in Jesus' name, Amen.

Questions

1) Do you have trouble relying on the support of others?

2) Did you know that when people help you, they gain a feeling of joy for being a blessing to others?

3) How can you rally support in your life or in the life of someone who is walking through a difficult time?

Enter God's promises with confidence!

DAY 10: FIVE MINUTES

"Yet the news about him spread all the more, so that crowds of people came to hear him and to be healed of their sicknesses. But Jesus often withdrew to lonely places and prayed" (Luke 5.15-16 NIV).

Every time my lead trainer taught me a new skill, he would have me learn it by doing five 5-minute rounds of training sessions with a minute break in between. If I was grappling, I had to do five 5-minute rounds. If I was practicing stand-up (punching, kicking, foot work, etc.), I had to do five 5-minute rounds. If I was doing cardio, I had to do five 5-minute rounds. Each of the five minutes was intense, and by the time I got to my last 5 minute round, I was exhausted. This thirty minute aggressive training session was tucked within a 2 – 3 hour workout.

Even though my body wanted to quit, I had to force it to move by the will of my mind. Once I finished my workout, my lead trainer had me sit for a 5-minute meditating session. These five minutes were pure bliss to me. While my eyes were closed, he would encourage me with all that I had learned. I would imagine myself perfectly executing every skill. Then, he would remain silent, so I could meditate freely. I would always meditate on God. I would confess His glory and praise Him for all that He has done for me, especially giving me Jesus. I would pray for myself and for my trainers. I would sit and fill my depleted body, mind and soul with His abundance.

By the time I opened my eyes, I felt rested, restored and rejuvenated, and it only took five minutes! Our lives are hectic and many times we are in seasons of intense pressing or brokenness; however, if we would only slip away for five minutes, we could find the strength to continue.

"But when you pray, go away by yourself, shut the door behind you, and pray to your Father in private. Then your Father, who sees everything, will reward you" (Matthew 6.6 NLT).

God, You know that my day-to-day obligations and my life's calling often leave me with very little time to seek restoration. I understand that You do give me seasons of rest, but during those busy times when everything seems to be falling apart, I know that I can slip away to a closet, a bathroom or my car and take five minutes to fill myself with Your abundant peace, joy and reassurance. Help me to remember to take a moment several times a day to seek You. I pray this in Jesus' name, Amen.

Questions

1) How can you slip away several times a day to spend time with God?

2) Can you rearrange your schedule to ensure that you are able to spend time reading your Bible and praying?

3) Did you know that when you spend time with God, you are empowered to effectively live for Him?

Take time to spend with God and watch your day transform!

DAY 11: THE MEEK

"But the meek will inherit the land and enjoy peace and prosperity" (Psalm 37.11 NIV).

Two men in the Bible were said to be meek: Moses and Jesus. When you look at the outcome of their lives, you realize that there is something important about meekness. In history, the term meek was used with war horses. When a horse would submit to its rider, they would become of one mind and body, and the power harnessed from that connection was almost unstoppable.

As a fighter, you really do not know how you will react in the ring/cage until your first fight. Some first-time fighters go crazy. They are unable to control their movements; and the skill, endurance and strength they acquired from months of training go out the window. Other fighters, however, stay focused, listen to their trainers and patiently wait for the right moments to react.

Before I got into my cage fight, I subdued all my emotions. I knew exactly where my trainers were, and I did everything they told me to do. When the fight went from stand-up to the floor, I listened for my new directions. When I took top mount, I kept my body under control for several seconds while my opponent twisted and pulled under me. Finally, when my trainers told me to strike, I did with all the strength and energy I had in me. When the fight was over, I fell to my knees and released all my emotions, thanking God for getting me through to the end.

God wants us to be meek, so He can pour His power into our lives. When we let go of the control and allow God to control and direct our lives, there is no stopping what He can do through us for His kingdom.

"Blessed are the meek, for they will inherit the earth" (Matthew 5.5 NIV).

God, I want my life to fulfill every purpose that You have for it, and I know that I'll only be able to achieve those victories if I'm submitted to Your authority. I want my life to have meaning. I want to make a difference for eternity. I know that I can't do it on my own. Please, guide and direct my life. Teach me to stay so sensitive to Your Spirit that I'll make the smallest adjustments and changes without hesitation. I pray this in Jesus' name, Amen.

Questions

1) Does the word "meek" seem counterculture to you?

2) How will creating a lifestyle of meekness transform your life?

3) Does giving control to God cause you to fear or does it encourage your faith?

Let God have the wheel and watch where He takes you!

DAY 12: BACK TO TRAINING

"I give them eternal life, and they will never perish. No one can snatch them away from me, for my Father has given them to me, and he is more powerful than anyone else. No one can snatch them from the Father's hand" (John 10.28-29 NLT).

When my husband saw me after I came home from my week long MMA training camp, he was not happy. I was bruised, tired and confused. I left my camp a day early because, quite frankly, I was scared. Training for a fight was on the opposite side of normal for me, and I really questioned whether it was God's will.

After I let go of my defenses, I knew in my spirit that God had called me into this strange world for a brief time; however, my husband had to go through his own period of struggling for understanding. The head of the production company contacted us, and my husband told him that I would no longer be training. I didn't argue with my husband because I knew that he loved me and he was concerned for my safety. If God wanted me to train, He would have to change my husband's mind. My husband is a Holy Spirit led man, and I trusted that he would do whatever God called him to do.

A couple of days later, my husband searched through the Bible and came to the part where Paul sent Onesimus back to his master. He felt God telling him to send me back to my training. So I continued training and gathered more bruises and injuries, but God gave us peace that we were doing His will. Although it is hard to send the people we hold dear into situations that are different, scary or even dangerous; we can trust that God will continue His sovereign will in their lives. Nothing or no one can snatch their spirits from God's hands once they have asked Jesus into their hearts and lives, and that truth should fill us with joy.

"I am sending him—who is my very heart—back to you" (Philemon 1.12 NIV).

God, I'm determined to trust You with the lives of those I love. I won't let fear stop me from allowing them to fulfill the purposes that You have for them. I know that You have never promised that we wouldn't experience hard times and pain, but You have promised us eternity with You in heaven; and no one can take that away from us. I pray this in Jesus' name, Amen.

Questions

1) Have you ever had to allow someone you love to walk into the "cage" of life?

2) Were you able to lean on God for support as the people you care about take hits from the world?

3) How do you think God feels when He watches the ones He loves suffer?

God will never let you go!

DAY 13: LIGHT AT THE GYM

"For God, who said, 'Let there be light in the darkness,' has made this light shine in our hearts so we could know the glory of God that is seen in the face of Jesus Christ" (2 Corinthians 4.6 NLT).

I am amazed by how many Christians I discovered in the world of Mix Martial Arts. Through choice or life circumstance, they found themselves in the ring or the cage; and they each had a fresh outlook on Jesus and faith. One Christ-follower encouraged me greatly. He is a pastor of a church, but he is also a chaplain for fighters. Before a fight, he goes to every room and speaks truth and love to each fighter.

I got to speak with him twice during the two most difficult times of my journey. He spoke to me while I cut weight the day of my weigh-in and just before my fight the following day. He had a perspective that I desperately needed. I didn't know how to live out my faith in an actual MMA fight, but since he had already walked down that path, he could be a light of understanding to me.

God loves and longs for all His children, and He will send His faithful servants to go get them wherever they may be. Since God also loves fighters, He has planted lamp posts in local rings and cages all across the globe. I finally got to see God's grace poured into an area that I had never experienced before. I am blessed to have a fuller view of God's love in action, and I am honored that He would trust me to be a light in the darkness for Him.

"The light shines in the darkness, and the darkness can never extinguish it" (John 1.5 NLT).

God, help me be a light to those who don't know You. I know that You care for all Your children in all areas of life, and You will put a passion in Your faithful servants to go get them. I want to be one of Your followers who earnestly brings others into an awesome relationship with You. I won't question Your methods. I just want You to send me. I pray this in Jesus' name, Amen.

Questions

1) How can you be a light in the darkness where you work and live?

2) What are some little ways that you can show love to people who may not know Jesus as their Lord and Savior?

3) Can you think of a time when someone reached into your pit of despair, shining the light of Jesus on your dark situation?

Let the light of Jesus shine in your life!

DAY 14: BREATH OF GOD

"I weep with sorrow; encourage me by your word" (Psalm 119.28 NLT).

During my MMA training, I felt like I was in a desert land of faith. At any moment, I could have given up and claimed defeat. When your capacity is stretched thin and you are walking a tightrope of trust, any little thing can break you and cause you to fold the whole situation up and throw it away.

Thankfully, God knew I had reached my limit, so He sent His encouragement to me through His Word. The Bible is a Living Force that affects people, books, music and a multitude of other forms of communication that become a buffering system in our walks of faith. I would drive to my next training session with all my injuries unhealed and sore, and I would hear a Christian song on the radio telling me not to give up. I would lie awake at night because my body ached and I couldn't move, and I would read a scripture about comfort and peace. I would question myself and wonder what I had gotten myself into, and my husband or my twin would have a verse of truth for me.

I had surrounded my life with the power of God's Word, and that is the only reason I made it through the fire that God called me to walk into. I believe many Christians are unable to fulfill God's will for their lives because they are not buffered with God's Word. We need to be reading it, listening to it and surrounding ourselves with people who are living it. The Bible is literally the breath of God pushing us to His best for our lives. Without it, we will never make it to our victories.

"So faith comes from hearing, and hearing through the word of Christ" (Romans 10.17 ESV).

God, I know that Your Word, the Bible, is the source of Your holy power, influencing our lives and our thinking for Your higher purposes and eternal vision. I put my trust in Your Word, and I want to surround myself with its authority and inspiration. I want to buffer my life with Truth, so that I can accomplish the plans that You have for me. I pray this in Jesus' name, Amen.

Questions

1) How can you add more of God's truth in your life through Christian movies, books, sermons, music, people, etc.?

2) Where do you go for support when you feel lost and confused?

3) Can you think of a time when God sent you a word of encouragement right when you needed it most?

Surround yourself with Godly influences!

DAY 15: ADRENALINE RUSH

"Seek the Kingdom of God above all else, and he will give you everything you need" (Luke 12.31 NLT).

I felt my chest crunch as my sparring partner barreled into me during our fourth 5-minute sparring session. I yelled out in pain, but I finished the five minutes. I knew something was wrong, but I wouldn't stop until I completed all five of my sparring rounds. After my fifth 5-minute spar was over, I quickly turned from the camera and looked at my chest. It appeared to be okay, and the sharp pain I felt on contact was gone. When the production team asked how I was doing, I told them that I was fine. But two hours later, I found myself at the E.R. and in a lot of pain.

I couldn't believe that I continued sparring even after I received excruciating chest contusions. This phenomenon happens a lot in contact sports, and it is known as an *adrenaline rush*. Many athletes accrue injuries while training or performing, but they don't feel them until hours later. The adrenaline coursing through their veins masks the pain, and the damage done isn't fully understood until they take time to rest.

In life we receive many blows that shake us, and in this age of fast communication and instant information, we are expected to know exactly how we feel at contact. But we can't be expected to understand the ramifications of our condition until we have taken time to consider what we are experiencing. We must pray and seek God's counsel before we make any statements, decisions or actions when going through major life changes and transitions. I have made it my rule to pray on something for at least three days before I make any movement because I don't want to alter my life when I can't fully comprehend the full weight of the situation.

"Don't worry about anything; instead, pray about everything. Tell God what you need, and thank him for all he has done" (Philippians 5.6 NLT).

God, thank You for showing me that I can wait before making any changes in my life. I know that people will respect my desire to seek Your counsel, and I will be better prepared to make the right decision. When my life is getting rushed and I'm confronted with several different directions, remind me to take time to find peace and clarity in You. I pray this in Jesus' name, Amen.

Questions

1) Have you ever made decisions during a hectic time only to regret your choices?

2) How can you begin to pray about everything before making any decisions?

3) Is there someone close to you that can keep you accountable to pray before reacting?

Pray about it first!

DAY 16: OVERLAPPING LEVELS

"But the gate is narrow (contracted by pressure) and the way is straitened and compressed that leads away to life, and few are those who find it" (Matthew 7.14 AMP).

I recently finished a season of fasting. I felt God calling me to all kinds of fasts—water only, Daniel Diet (fruits and veggies only), liquids only, no coffee, and a year of no meats. God taught me a lot about His character, He exposed much of my hidden sin and He performed many beautiful miracles during my fasts. However, my meat fast overlapped with my MMA training.

I had one month left to go of my fast when I started training, and I was worried that I wouldn't be able to finish. But I knew God called me to do one year because I waited for His affirmation before I started. God had taken away my desire for meat three days before I dedicated myself to fasting a year. I shouldn't have doubted God, though, because I was able to finish my last month, and my training wasn't affected.

I've experienced this phenomenon many times—I call it *overlapping levels*. I've noticed that before God moves you to your next level, there is a period of overlapping that may push you to your limit and cause you to doubt. It feels like your circumstances can't contain your expanding capacity, like a family who has outgrown their home. This short time of intense pressure is a good indicator that God is about to move you; so instead of doubting or complaining, just thank God for squeezing you into the next phase of His plan for your life.

"Humble yourselves, therefore, under God's mighty hand, that he may lift you up in due time" (1 Peter 5.6 NIV).

God, thank You for letting me be aware of the unique movement of Your will. I don't want to complain or doubt You, so knowing that a season of pressure foreshadows some kind of release or change, encourages me to maintain the course with joy. I pray that I experience many seasons of overlapping levels as I continue on the purpose You've created for me. I pray this in Jesus' name, Amen.

Questions

1) Have you ever experienced a time of immense pressure just before God released you into new territory?

2) Does the squeeze into a new level of faith with God intimidate or excite you?

3) What can you do to help make those times of transition in your life easier to handle?

A squeeze in life means a change in scenery!

DAY 17: ROLL WITH THE PUNCHES

"Do you not know that in a race all the runners run, but only one gets the prize? Run in such a way as to get the prize" (1 Corinthians 9.24 NIV).

When I was training for MMA, I got hit on the ridge of my nose; which caused a nice, blue bump to appear right where my sunglasses rest. The next time I sparred, I was scared to get hit in the face because of my injury. My trainers were not happy that I kept flinching and turning away. In order to remedy my fear, they had my sparring partner punch me ten times in the face.

Flash forward to a month later when I was "rolling" (doing floor work or Jiu-Jitsu) with a friend of mine who volunteered to be my "body" (a person who allows you to practice floor technique on her). My hands slipped out of my grip, and I landed a hit to her face–right on the ridge of her nose. Instantly, she got a hematoma that swelled and turned blue. I waited for her reaction. I knew it had hurt because I received the exact injury.

Instead of allowing the pain to cause her to turn away or flinch, she used the injury as a reason to keep going. She knew that training for a fight was painful, but it was also exciting, exhilarating and challenging. She loved the thrill of it all, and a hit to the face was part of the adventure.

After I saw her reaction, I had to eat a big slice of humble pie on camera. I said that God was showing me that I needed to fix my attitude. Life is an adventure, and we can't allow the injuries along the way to stop us from doing our best. The bigger the battle, the bigger the bumps and bruises; and we need to take the hits and keep running strong. Nothing worth fighting for is ever easy.

"We can rejoice, too, when we run into problems and trials, for we know that they help us develop endurance. And endurance develops strength of character, and character strengthens our confident hope of salvation" (Romans 5.3-4 NLT).

God, I know that I'm going to take hits during my race toward eternity, but I want to take them with grace and confidence. I trust that You won't let me experience any injury that will cause me to quit. I'm determined to be a strong warrior for You, and I won't back down from the challenges that You lay before me. I pray this in Jesus' name, Amen.

Questions

1) Have you ever been humbled by the positive attitude of others?

2) How can you maintain a good attitude even during difficulty?

3) Do you believe that you have control over how you feel in difficult situations?

Make up your mind to stay positive!

DAY 18: THOSE CRAZY PROPHETS

"Son of man, your people talk about you in their houses and whisper about you at the doors. They say to each other, 'Come on, let's go hear the prophet tell us what the LORD is saying!'" (Ezekiel 33:30 NLT).

While I trained for MMA, I constantly told God how strange I felt and how weird I must look to others. It is not every day that a Christian mother and writer trains to be a MMA fighter. I knew people would judge or misunderstand me, but there really wasn't much I could do about it. I was submitted to the authority of the Holy Spirit, and I continued to pray for guidance at every turn.

I definitely wasn't perfect, but I was faithful. During this time, I was reading through the Bible for my third time; and I happened to be reading the Major Prophets. God asked them do the craziest things that made my little steps of faith look like a normal day at the park, including walking around naked and barefoot for three years (Isa 20.3), lying down for 390 days (Ezek 4.4-5), wearing a yoke around the neck (Jer 27.2), cooking food over human excrement (Ezek 4.12), hiding underwear under rocks (Jer 13.4) and shaving the head and throwing the hair into the wind (Ezek 5.2).

Talk about weird! But God needed to make a statement to a stubborn and rebellious nation, and it took crazy, out of the norm things to get their attention. God wanted everyone to hear His Word through His messengers, and He knew that news travels the fastest when it's unexpected. Reading the stories of the prophets made me feel a lot better because I knew that I was in good company, and I was very happy that God didn't ask me to walk around naked or shave my head.

"Trust in the Lord with all your heart, and do not lean on your own understanding. In all your ways acknowledge him, and he will make straight your paths" (Proverbs 3.5-6 ESV).

God, You desire to send Your grace to a nation that has forgotten You, so many times You will call Your faithful servants to do crazy things to get their attention. I know that Your understanding is beyond my comprehension, and I don't want to doubt Your will. Help me to faithfully stay obedient to Your movement even when it sounds a little crazy. I pray this in Jesus' name, Amen.

Questions

1) Has God ever asked you to do something that didn't make sense to a human perspective?

2) How does living by faith encourage your reliance on God?

3) Did God surprise you with an amazing outcome when you decided to trust Him in your situation?

Walk by faith, not by sight!

DAY 19: WEIGHT OF OUR BEST

"Work willingly at whatever you do, as though you were working for the Lord rather than for people" (Colossians 3.23 NLT).

Weight is very important in MMA fighting. Competitors can be diverse in size and height, but they must be proportionate in weight. There is a fine science to cutting weight, and it is definitely not for the faint of heart. When I was told that I would have to get down to 126 pounds, I was worried. I'm 5' 7" with an athletic build, and I haven't weighed 126 pounds since junior high. In the past, I've fasted—drinking only water—for 10 days, and I got down to 128lbs and that was with no food in my body and no extra muscle mass from the strenuous exercise of MMA training.

I prayed to God about my concerns, but I felt Him telling me to press on. The final week leading up to my fight, I did everything I could humanly do to lose weight. I continued working out twice a day and drastically cut my calories. Then, the day before my fight I cut weight in the sauna—sitting for 60 minutes (6 increments of 10 minutes) in the dry heat. Even after all that, I was still over!

That evening I went to my weigh-in. It is a huge embarrassment to the fighters and the trainers if they don't make weight. I got on the scale and held my breath. I weighed 126 pounds and some ounces. It was a miracle! That's one thing I've learned about miracles—many times we have to do everything in the natural for God to do His supernatural. We have to give God our best, so He will give us the rest.

"They triumphed over him by the blood of the Lamb and by the word of their testimony; they did not love their lives so much as to shrink from death" (Revelation 12.11 NIV).

God, I want a life that is marked by miracles, but I know that I have to be all in. I understand that doing my best will not be easy and many times I will want to quit, but I trust that You will shape my circumstances and add Your supernatural touches when I'm at the end of my strength, talent and resources. I pray this in Jesus' name, Amen.

Questions

1) Is there a time when you gave all you could in the natural, yet you still needed God to provide in the supernatural?

2) How has God showed up in the little areas of obedience in your life?

3) Has there been a time when God saved you from shame and embarrassment?

Give God your best, and He'll do the rest!

DAY 20: MINISTRY OF THE HOME

"But those who won't care for their relatives, especially those in their own household, have denied the true faith. Such people are worse than unbelievers" (1 Timothy 5.8 NLT).

The two months I trained for my MMA fight were very difficult on my family and me. My husband and my kids sacrificed a lot to allow me to commit to the many hours and the physical, emotional and mental demands of preparing for a fight. In retrospect, I realize that there would have been no way I could have trained if my house hadn't been in order.

I think so many times we ask God to expand our territory and to give us more responsibility, but we aren't disciplined and joyful with the responsibilities He's already given us. If we are not generously and enthusiastically serving in the ministry of being a spouse and parent, why would God give us another ministry?

In all honesty, it is a lot easier and more enjoyable to wash the dishes, help my kids with homework and spend intimate time with my husband than it is to take a punch, kick a bag and to workout until I want to throw-up. If doing laundry means that I get to care for an amazing family of five, then I will gladly do it! Every blessing comes with a burden. Once we have a godly perspective about all the blessings we've been given, and we are strong enough to handle the burdens that come with them, God will see fit to give us more influence at the appropriate time.

"Whoever can be trusted with very little can also be trusted with much, and whoever is dishonest with very little will also be dishonest with much" (Luke 16.10 NIV).

God, I know You won't expand my influence if I'm already struggling and complaining about the responsibilities You have already blessed me with. I don't want to fake my joy and enthusiasm; rather, I want to truly love and value the ministry of the home. I realize that it is an amazing honor to serve those closest to me. I pray this in Jesus' name, Amen.

Questions

1) How have you sacrificed for the ministry of the home?

2) Did you know that everything you do for your family is valuable to the Lord?

3) How does the cultural world-view of the home differ from God's view of the home?

Ministry starts in the home!

DAY 21: THE GOOD FIGHT

"I have fought the good fight, I have finished the race, I have kept the faith" (2 Timothy 4.7 NIV).

While I trained, I was able to fly to Florida to see an actual MMA bout. I followed an up and coming female fighter who ranked in the top five of her weight class. I got to see behind the scene of her weigh-in, and I watched her prepare for her fight the next day. I sat in her corner during the fight. And I stood center stage with her when she won by decision. The entire fighting championship was surreal, exciting and overwhelming; but my favorite part was watching the fighter prepare for her fight—physically, mentally, emotionally and spiritually.

What intrigued me most was how peaceful she was. I couldn't believe that someone who was about to walk into the cage could be so at ease. Almost two months later, I found myself in her shoes. I was getting ready for a fight in front of thousands of people, and I was completely at peace—kind of like being in the eye of the storm. When I thought about how calm I was, I remembered the fighter I had met before her bout; and I finally understood.

When you train hard—pouring all of your heart, strength and energy into preparing for your fight—you are left with no regrets and with a firm knowledge that you are ready. Win or lose—you've held nothing back. There is immense peace in knowing that you gave it your all. God has called us into this cage of faith called life, and we need to fight the good fight for Him. When we prepare and give Him our best, He is able to accomplish the impossible through us and in our lives.

"Jesus looked at them and said, 'With man this is impossible, but with God all things are possible'" (Matthew 19.26 NIV).

God, I don't want to end my life with regret. I don't want to squander the time you have given me living a mediocre and marginal existence. I promise to give You my all, and I trust that You will take my little life and make it into something beautiful and inspiring. I pray this in Jesus' name, Amen.

Questions

1) How has God been able to give you peace in the storms of your life?

2) Was there a time in your life that you chose to have faith instead of fear when facing a difficulty?

3) Do you think God is pleased when you choose to remain peaceful during difficult times?

Claim peace in the midst of chaos!

DAY 22: VOICE OF THE ENEMY

"Jesus turned and said to Peter, 'Get behind me, Satan! You are a stumbling block to me; you do not have in mind the concerns of God, but merely human concerns'" (Matthew 16.23 NIV).

God has a plan for our lives, but that plan can easily become distorted by the many voices in this world, including our own. When I filmed the reality show, there were a lot of people who had many ideas about how the show should develop. I found myself confused by the many thoughts, opinions and reactions to the steps I was taking.

Everyone's viewpoint was valid and well-meaning; however, valid and well-meaning can still be the opposite of God's will. I am reminded of when Peter insisted that Jesus not allow Himself to be tortured and murdered (Matt 16.22). Although Peter's response is well-meaning, Jesus called Peter the voice of the Enemy. Jesus knew that God's plan for Him was to die on the cross for the world's sins, and Peter didn't comprehend the eternal movement that he was eager to destroy.

Most people including myself have very valid points-of-view, but we must remember to always seek God's will. I often tell people before giving them advice not to write my words with gold on their hearts. I would hate for seemingly helpful opinions to cause God's people to miss out on what He has for them. Unless we allow the Holy Spirit to work through our mouths, our voice can be a tool for the Enemy. We must always be careful about seeking God before voicing our thoughts, and we can take care to seek advice from people who are directed by the Holy Spirit.

"But the Helper, the Holy Spirit, whom the Father will send in my name, he will teach you all things and bring to your remembrance all that I have said to you" (John 14.26 ESV).

God, I don't want to give out well-meaning advice that contradicts Your eternal plan. Help me to choose my words prayerfully according to how the Holy Spirit leads me. Also, give me discernment, so I can separate advice that is Holy Spirit inspired from advice that is not. I pray this in Jesus' name, Amen.

Questions

1) When you are concerned with only God's opinion, how does that free you from the opinions of others?

2) Has there been a time when people were let down by your decisions because you decided to obey the voice of the Lord?

3) How can you learn to focus more on what God thinks and less on what the world thinks?

Seek God and He will make your path straight!

DAY 23: POWER OF THE TONGUE

"The tongue has the power of life and death, and those who love it will eat its fruit" (Proverbs 18.21 NIV).

When I started training to be a MMA fighter, I knew almost nothing about that sport. Every time I would try to perform a move, I would do it wrong. I stood wrong, moved wrong, punched wrong, kicked wrong, grappled wrong—you name it, I did it wrong! Because this sport is already extremely demanding, starting from ground zero left me with very little to be encouraged about.

I felt defeated, and if it hadn't been for life-giving words spoken over me, I would have probably quit. The Bible says that the tongue has the power to give life or death, and I was blessed to be surrounded by people who spoke life. My trainers encouraged me after every grueling training session. My pastors encouraged me every time I ran into them. My family and friends encouraged me when they saw me. My husband and twin sister encouraged me continuously.

And, most of all, the Holy Spirit encouraged me. I tuned my ears to the fruits of their words and shut out all naysayers. Whenever God calls us into unknown territory that stretches our faith and resolve, we need to look for those encouraging words that will pave the way to our success and ignore the words that are out to destroy us.

"Don't use foul or abusive language. Let everything you say be good and helpful, so that your words will be an encouragement to those who hear them" (Ephesian 4.29 NLT).

God, help me to be an uplifter of people's dreams. If the Holy Spirit is directing someone on a difficult path, I want to be a voice of support and empowerment. Also, train my ears to hear Your whispers of approval, and help me to focus on the encouragers and not on the discouragers. I pray this in Jesus' name, Amen.

Questions

1) Did you know that there is great power in your thoughts and words?

2) How can you pave a path of victory with your word choice?

3) Are there negative thoughts that you need to clean from your heart, mind and mouth?

Jesus died to give you victory, so claim it today!

DAY 24: A VALUED PEOPLE

"Now if we are children, then we are heirs—heirs of God and co-heirs with Christ, if indeed we share in his sufferings in order that we may also share in his glory" (Romans 8.17 NIV).

I've learned that we judge people based on our own perceptions of importance. We put people on a pedestal or in a ditch, depending on how they rank in our skewed understanding of hierarchy. However, God loves everyone equally. He places the highest value on each of us, which He demonstrated when He left His glory, came to this earth as a man and died for us on the cross.

I thought I had gotten a handle on my hidden sin of judging until I started filming for the reality TV show. All of a sudden, I was anxious and nervous about what the "show" people thought, and I put them on pedestals. This caused me to struggle because I began to worry more about their view of me than God's view of me. I thought more about pleasing them than God. The funny thing is that they never asked to be on pedestals; but because their world was new and prestigious to me, I automatically ranked them high.

However, I realized that if we honor God above all else, we won't judge and rank people because God truly outweighs us all. I won't worry about what other people say, think, do or want because I'm too consumed with what the Creator says, thinks, does and wants. Life is so simple when we put God first—He stays on the pedestal, He throws our sin in the ditch and we all become co-heirs with Christ.

"Do not judge others, and you will not be judged. For you will be treated as you treat others. The standard you use in judging is the standard by which you will be judged" (Matthew 7.1-2 NLT).

God, no matter what new circumstance I find myself in or what new group of people I rub elbows with, I want to always put You first. I won't be nervous or intimidated by others because I know that we are all equal in Your eyes. You put a priceless value on us all, and You love us so much that You willing took the ugliness of our sins. Thank You. I pray this in Jesus' name, Amen.

Questions

1) Have you unknowingly judged people by placing them on a pedestal or in a ditch with your thoughts?

2) Has anyone ever mistaken your humility for inferiority?

3) How does honoring God above all else help you to have a healthier perspective of others?

Value others and yourself as children of God!

DAY 25: POST OF FAITH

"Be on your guard; stand firm in the faith; be courageous; be strong" (1 Corinthians 16.13 NIV).

In my fight, I got top mount and posted (keeping my body rigid) over my opponent for several seconds. I kept my knees tight around her hips and my arms square over her head. Though she wiggled, punched and moved, I kept my body unbending and followed her every movement. I wouldn't let her roll or get out of my grip.

She slowly wore herself out and became open to an offensive attack. Posting takes a lot of patience, resilience and focus. *Patience* because you have to wait for your opponent to exhaust herself; *Resilience* because you can't react even though you're getting hit; *Focus* because your opponent is trying to free herself, so you must counter her attempts. In life, we will find ourselves in the ring with our circumstance, and threats of disbelief and fear will try to drag us down or cause our defeat.

When we are experiencing a season of difficulty, instead of fighting back, many times we may need to post in our faith. We can stay patient in our faith, resilient in our faith and focused in our faith; and allow our circumstances to wear out. Our faith can be a buffer that saves us from falling victim to the trials, temptations and tests of life. So the next time you become aware that an opponent has just stepped in the cage with you, just post in your faith and wait for the Master Trainer to tell you what to do next.

"Wait for the LORD; be strong and take heart and wait for the LORD" (Psalm 27.14 NIV).

God, I know that there are times to act and there are times to wait and stand firm, and I ask that You show me which route to take when I find myself in a confrontation. Life is filled with many battles, and I believe that You know the path to my victory. I want to trust You and wait courageously in my faith for You to respond in my situation. I pray this in Jesus' name, Amen.

Questions

1) How can having patience during a difficult season of life prevent you from making rash decisions?

2) Is there a time that you reacted to a situation only to find that your actions caused more tension?

3) Can you learn to stay resilient and focused during times of trouble, so you are better able to hear God's direction?

Don't react to your situation; rather, act on God's Word!

DAY 26: UNSEEN GREATNESS

"The eyes of the Lord search the whole earth in order to strengthen those whose hearts are fully committed to him...." (2 Chronicles 16.9 NLT).

Making a reality TV show had its perks. Everywhere I went people were so obliging. Everyone would see the TV crew, and they would do whatever it took to accommodate our needs. I like to think that I'm special, but the main reason people went above and beyond to help us was because of the show. I know that I personally worked harder and sacrificed more, believing that my actions and words may someday be displayed on national TV.

I wanted to be the best wife, the best mom, the best Christian, the best athlete and the best person that I could be. But what happens when the camera crew is not there? Will I continue to pour all my energy into the seemingly insignificant details of life when no one is looking? Will I try to do my best and not compromise even if I don't have an audience? As Christians, we must remember that God is always watching us.

I know this truth may sound cliché, but His eyes see everything, and He is always looking on this earth for hearts that are dedicated to Him. God will show Himself strong on our behalf, but we need to live every moment like we are in the presence of a King. He is the only audience that truly matters.

"The Lord looks down from heaven and sees the whole human race. From his throne he observes all who live on the earth. He made their hearts, so he understands everything they do" (Psalm 33.13-15 NLT).

God, I don't want to live a deceived life. I want my words and actions to be the same whether I'm in a crowd or in my home. If I allow myself to have double standards, I will never have a pure heart for You. My deceptions will hurt me, those I love and my witness for Christ. Reveal to me any mismatched and impure actions in my life. I pray this in Jesus' name, Amen.

Questions

1) Does knowing that God is always with you help you to work diligently unto the Lord even when no one is looking?

2) Have you ever found yourself working harder when people are watching?

3) Did you know that the sacrifices that you make in private are just as important as the sacrifices that you make in public?

God sees all the hard work that you do in secret!

DAY 27: FLAWED BUT CONFIDENT

"Each time he said, 'My grace is all you need. My power works best in weakness.' So now I am glad to boast about my weaknesses, so that the power of Christ can work through me" (2 Corinthians 12.9 NLT).

During a significantly tense moment while filming for the reality show, I got angry with one of the producers. I felt like I was being set up for a disappointment, and I blamed her for letting me down. Of course, she had nothing to do with what happened. She was just an innocent bystander caught in the crossfire who just so happened to be holding a camera.

I immediately said sorry, and I felt heavy with regret. This particular producer had been on my heart, and I had been praying for her and talking with her about Christ. I was upset at myself for blowing it so terribly. I talked with her about my mistake later that day, and she understood and even empathized with me. I apologized again, and let her know that I felt bad about my actions.

She seemed to appreciate my sincerity, and life went on as usual. As a Christian, I sometimes feel this need to be perfect, but I'm not perfect and never will be. However, I'm beginning to realize that people don't want perfect; they want honest. They want to see a flawed person walk in confidence while simultaneously admitting her mistakes and shortcomings. Nobody is perfect, and that should encourage us to base our self-esteem on God's perfection not our own. Only through Jesus are we made righteous before God.

"This righteousness is given through faith in Jesus Christ to all who believe...." (Romans 3.22 NIV).

God, I know that I will never be perfect, and I'm determined to have a keen understanding of my strengths and weaknesses. I want to be able to freely admit when I did a great job and when I blew it. No one is exempt from making mistakes, but only a handful become graceful at admitting and apologizing for them. I will remain confident that Your power will shine in my weakness. I pray this in Jesus' name, Amen.

Questions

1) Do you think it is scary or comforting to know that you will never be perfect?

2) How does humility in your mistakes help others to be honest about their shortcomings?

3) After you stumble, can you confidently get back up again and continue to walk in the grace of God?

Grab hold of God's grace and continue your walk of faith!

DAY 28: MOTIVATING OTHERS

"Dear children, let's not merely say that we love each other; let us show the truth by our actions" (1 John 3.18 NLT).

My husband has lost twenty-five pounds since my fight. We've known each other since high school, and in college people called us the "work-out couple." All my husband's young life, he could eat pretty much anything he wanted without gaining weight. But as we aged into our thirties, his once athletic lifestyle took a backseat to his busy work schedule; and his eating habits stayed similar to that of a twenty-year-old.

For over five years, he has wanted to lose weight and get into shape, but he lacked the motivation in that area. I've tried to help and encourage him, but we must all individually take responsibility for our own health. Something happened, though, when he saw me train for my fight. He watched me push myself during my workouts and spars, and he realized he had no more excuses.

Ever since then, he has killed the spirit of gluttony in his life. Little did I know that God would use my crazy act of obedience in the cage to change the course of my husband's life. His transformation is worth it all, and I'm glad that I could give back a little of the inspiration that he has given me. Together, we encourage each other to give our best to God!

"So, whether you eat or drink, or whatever you do, do all to the glory of God" (1 Corinthians 10.31 ESV).

God, we don't realize who is watching us when we are obediently following Your will. Our stretches of faith and our pushes of determination have purpose, and You will use them to influence the lives of many, especially those closest to us. Thank You for using my obedience to motivate my husband. I'm grateful to have a relationship with my husband where we both can encourage each other. I pray this in Jesus' name, Amen.

Questions

1) Do you struggle with food or with any other addiction that prevents you from experiencing God's best in your life?

2) Did you know that the Holy Spirit will give you strength to find freedom from your personal strongholds?

3) Can you make a decision today to no longer be ruled by an addiction, so that God will always have the highest place in your heart?

Submit to God, and He will give you the strength to overcome!

DAY 29: THE FAITHFUL GRIND

"If you are faithful in little things, you will be faithful in large ones. But if you are dishonest in little things, you won't be honest with greater responsibilities" (Luke 16.10 NLT).

I've exercised all my adult life. During my "baby making season," I really had to stay focused on maintaining a healthy lifestyle. After each of my three babies, I had at least 30 pounds to lose. Trying to get back into pre-pregnancy shape is very difficult and takes lots of determination. It took me a full year of diligence to lose the weight once my husband and I brought each of our babies home.

I stayed faithful at protecting my health because I know God calls us to be good stewards of our temples (bodies). If I hadn't been faithful at working-out and watching my calories, I wouldn't have been victorious in following God into the cage. I would have missed that entire segment of life that God had prepared for me.

So many times we want to do great things for God, but we aren't staying faithful to the everyday tasks He calls us to, but it is the little things that truly matter. Eventually the small decisions we make each day will add up, and we will find ourselves either ready or unprepared for God's best in our lives. Let us continue doing our best for God every day, knowing that He will bless our obedience.

"Don't you realize that your body is the temple of the Holy Spirit, who lives in you and was given to you by God? You do not belong to yourself, for God bought you with a high price. So you must honor God with your body" (1 Corinthians 6.19-20 NLT).

God, help me to stay faithful to the seemingly insignificant details of life. I know that my daily decisions influence the power and purpose of my entire walk of faith. I trust that my day-to-day faithfulness will eventually add up to be something spectacular for Your Kingdom. I pray this in Jesus' name, Amen.

Questions

1) Is there an area of your life that you have become lazy or that you have neglected?

2) Did you know that it only takes one decision to change a situation in your life?

3) What can you do today to begin to turn around an area of your life that you know needs improvement?

Look to God, and He can restore your circumstance!

DAY 30: KINGDOM GAIN

"Here's the lesson: Use your worldly resources to benefit others and make friends. Then, when your earthly possessions are gone, they will welcome you to an eternal home" (Luke 16.9 NLT).

As my fight day approached, I would focus on the time when the fight was over, and I would finally be freed from the burden. Win or lose, I simply wanted to be on the other side of my time in the cage. My fight was a blur. I was so nervous and emotionally charged that I couldn't really embrace the win I had achieved.

I know my family and friends were excited and proud of me, but I didn't know what an outsider thought—just someone from the crowd. What did they think of the female fighter who talked about God from center stage after her win? As my husband and I walked to our car to drive away from my stint as a MMA fighter, we saw two men getting into a sports car. The men looked liked urban professionals in their forties who were enjoying a guys' night out.

When they saw me in the parking lot, they immediately closed their car doors, walked straight over to me and each shook my hand. They didn't say a word as they headed back to their car. I'm glad God gave me that very special gesture of affirmation. I did His will and earned the respect of strangers. I stayed obedient to the Lord, and he kept me from shame.

"But the Lord God helps me; therefore I have not been disgraced; therefore I have set my face like a flint, and I know that I shall not be put to shame" (Isaiah 50.7 ESV).

God, I know that You want us to use our resources, gifts, talents and achievements to touch the lives of the lost, so they can start a relationship with You. You give us a platform, so we can have a godly influence on others. I pray that I always give You the glory and that I use up all my earthly advantages to further Your kingdom. I pray this in Jesus' name, Amen.

Questions

1) Have you experienced a time when others saw and respected your work for the Lord?

2) Did you know that though the world might not understand your devotion to God, they can appreciate your faithfulness?

3) Do you believe that God will shine His glory through your life when you take steps of obedience that scare you a little?

Risk it all for God, and He will establish your steps!

DAY 31: GOD CONNECTIONS

"Don't you know that you yourselves are God's temple and that God's Spirit lives in you?" (1 Corinthians 3.16 NIV).

When I first met my female MMA trainer, she wanted to know everything about me. She asked me a ton of questions and in turn revealed much about herself. She invited my husband and me out to dinner, and she came to our home so she could visit with my family. She wanted to meet everyone, and she went out of her way to have individual time with each person.

I was surprised by her eagerness to make friends because she would only be with us for a short time. She willingly connected with my family members, other MMA fighters, TV producers and people from my church. It didn't matter their age, profession, gender or ethnicity; if they were in her path, she would introduce herself. It was obvious she placed great value on people and relationships.

I learned a lot from watching my trainer. I realized that when God puts people in our lives—no matter who they are or how long they are there—He wants us to reach out to them. If God's Spirit lives in us, He will use us as an extension of His arm to share His love, mercy and favor to His beloved people.

> "Therefore, whenever we have the opportunity, we should do good to everyone—especially to those in the family of faith" (Galatians 6.10 NLT).

God, I know that there are no coincidences. You have mapped out who and when people will come in and out of my life. I don't want to miss an opportunity to reach out to others, and I trust that You will guide my actions and words. Help me to always be ready to introduce myself when Your Spirit has arranged a divine appointment. I pray this in Jesus' name, Amen.

Questions

1) Do you believe that God hand-picked the people in your life?

2) How can you touch the lives of the people closest to you?

3) Who in your life can you take time to get to know better today?

Touch the lives of the people in your life!

DAY 32: DEER FEET

"He makes me as surefooted as a deer, enabling me to stand on mountain heights" (Psalm 18.33 NLT).

My first day training with my lead MMA coach was eye opening. The seemingly trivial things, like standing, walking and turning were all different and strange. I had to position and move my body in a totally new way. My coach showed me how to walk, and I remember thinking that his feet looked like the feet of a deer.

He stepped on the balls of his feet, so at any moment he could change direction. Also, he never crossed his feet because that would expose his body to falling over easily. I had to practice over and over again to be able to walk like a deer. The day before my fight, my twin sister called me with a verse that God had given her for me. Psalm 18 was written by King David, and it is all about preparing for battle.

I especially loved the part of the verse that promised we would be "surefooted as a deer." I know that God will always prepare my feet for the battle He has placed before me. Whether I am wearing high heels, running shoes, work boots or no shoes—God is readying my feet to stand on "mountain heights" of victory. God knows that I will use that platform to bring the Good News of Jesus to others.

> "How beautiful on the mountains are the feet of those who bring good news, who proclaim peace, who bring good tidings, who proclaim salvation, who say to Zion, 'Your God reigns!'" (Isaiah 52.7 NIV).

God, I know that the "mountain heights" you have for us will not be easy to scale, but I also trust that you will prepare our feet for the climb. You call us to victories that are difficult and scary, but I know from first-hand experience that once we make it to the top, the view of understanding and faith surrounding us is life-changing. I'm willing to work hard because I want to proclaim the peace of Jesus to the world. I pray this in Jesus' name, Amen.

Questions

1) Have you ever had to start at the bottom of a new situation?

2) Are you able to sympathize with people who are just beginning a new path in life?

3) How will your humility help you to be more willing to start new adventures in your life?

It's never too late to start something new!

DAY 33: MY TWIN, THE BODY

"When I am with those who are weak, I share their weakness, for I want to bring the weak to Christ. Yes, I try to find common ground with everyone, doing everything I can to save some" (1 Corinthians 9.22 NLT).

I almost lost my twin sister in a car accident many years ago. Getting that phone call in the middle of the night was one of the worst experiences of my life. She wrestled through months of recovery and today has thriving health. However, her body does have some residual pain and is adorned with many scars, including a large one down her hip and leg where the doctors bolted her shattered hip back together.

I called her while I was training. I needed "a body." MMA fighters must practice their moves on others. These selfless people allow their bodies to be painfully manipulated and hit so that the fighters can improve their technique. My sister met me at the gym, and for about an hour I ran toward her body, locked my arms around her calves and used my shoulders and neck to knock her down. I did hold back a little bit.

I kept moving my hands to her hips, trying to help her land softly on the mat. I didn't want to hurt her, but I did. The next day she had bruises along her thick scar and her body hurt all over. Sometimes we can be so focused on what we need to get done that we forget that other people have pain and weaknesses that should not be exposed to our personal challenges. During my training, I leaned on my sister for many things, but that was the first and last time I used her as a body for training.

"Do nothing out of selfish ambition or vain conceit. Rather, in humility value others above yourselves, not looking to your own interests but each of you to the interests of the others" (Philippians 2.3-4 NIV).

God, help me to always be aware of the trials, hurts and weaknesses of others. I want to focus so much on serving others that I will never selflessly hurt them or hinder their walks of faith. I know how easy it is to get caught up in our own lives, especially when we are in a season of difficulty; but I want to stay aligned with Jesus' example: He never once took His eyes off a people who desperately needed a Savior. I pray this in Jesus' name, Amen.

Questions

1) Have you ever leaned on someone in a situation who was unable to bear the weight of the burden?

2) How will your daily interaction with the Lord help you to find strength to continue walking in obedience?

3) Did you ever have to carry the weight of someone else's problems that you felt incapable of handling?

Give your worries to God, for He cares about you!

DAY 34: MISSING FAMILY

"For everything there is a season, a time for every activity under heaven" (Ecclesiastes 3.1 NLT).

Training for a MMA fight took a huge chunk of time out of my schedule. Toward the end of my training, I had to work out in the mornings and spar in the evenings. Luckily my kids were in summer camp in the mornings, but arranging help in the evenings became difficult for me. I had two weeks left to train, and I longed to have my family time back. I was so unsure of everything at this point because I always prided myself on being a mother who always put her kids first.

All of a sudden, however, I found myself in a crazy, short season of becoming a MMA fighter. I told God that I was struggling, and I prayed for clarity. I took my kids to their church summer camp, and the teachers told me that they would be having Vacation Bible School (VBS) the following week for three hours every evening. I couldn't believe it. The church was close to the gym; so I was able to drop off my kids, train and then pick them right back up.

God not only provided the time required for me to train, but He also affirmed my steps of obedience by putting my kids in an atmosphere where they would learn more about Him! When we walk by faith into areas that make us feel unsure, God will clear the way so we can trust His leading. I'm thankful that God helped me through a very difficult stage of sacrifice, but I'm especially thankful that my training season is over and my family time is back to normal.

"Children are a gift from the Lord; they are a reward from him" (Psalm 127.3 NLT).

God, thank You for getting me through that short season of sacrifice. I now have such a profound joy in doing the simplest tasks required to maintain my family and home. I am honored to wash the dishes, fold the laundry and tuck warm, little bodies into bed every night. I don't take the role of being a parent and spouse lightly, and I feel immensely blessed to serve those I love. I pray this in Jesus' name, Amen.

Questions

1) Has there been a season in your life that took great sacrifice for your entire family?

2) Do you believe that God will not allow you to be in a situation that you cannot handle?

3) How has the difficult times in your life given you a better perspective of how you are truly blessed?

A quick walk in shadows makes the sun shine brighter!

DAY 35: TALKING ABOUT GOD

"Good comes from a good man because of the riches he has in his heart. Sin comes from a sinful man because of the sin he has in his heart. The mouth speaks of what the heart is full of" (Luke 6.45 NLV).

While filming for my reality show, I had to do a lot of interviews. It seemed that the interviews took up just as much time as my MMA training did. During my intimate camera chats, I almost always talked about God. I didn't have to force my faith-talks for the camera because I pulled from the thoughts that were already stored up in my heart. My twin sister told the camera in one of her interviews, "Alisa talks about God a lot, and it doesn't matter who she is talking to."

There was once a time in my life when I was scared to talk about God. When I saw an opportunity to share my faith, I would get uncomfortable and embarrassed. I felt out of sorts telling others about my relationship with Christ because it was very personal to me. But since I've set my heart on knowing Him and reading His Word, I can't help but talk about God and my faith if I find an audience that is willing to listen.

As Christians, we must store up God's truth in our hearts. We need to spend time talking to God through prayer, meditating on what the Holy Spirit is teaching us and reading God's Truth in the Bible. When we begin to fill our minds and hearts with God, the wisdom, grace and mercy of His nature will pour easily from our lips.

"Peace I leave with you; my peace I give you. I do not give to you as the world gives. Do not let your hearts be troubled and do not be afraid" (John 14.27 NIV).

God, I want to discuss my relationship with You like I discuss all the other details of my life. Teach me Your amazing mysteries and help me gain Your wisdom, so the world will long for the joy and peace that I experience in You. Fill me so completely with the Holy Spirit that my thoughts, actions and words overflow with Your presence and truth. Let the world see my passion for all things eternal, so that they too will find the hope and salvation that I have in Christ. I pray this in Jesus' name, Amen.

Questions

1) Are you storing up God's Word in your heart?

2) Do you believe that every effort you make to read the Bible will benefit your life and the lives of those around you?

3) Can you share something that the Holy Spirit has shown you to someone in your life today?

When God is in your thoughts, He'll show up in your words!

DAY 36: CROPS DON'T DISAPPEAR

"So do not throw away this confident trust in the Lord. Remember the great reward it brings you!" (Hebrews 10.35 NLT).

When the main producer of the reality show called me, he sounded nervous. He told me that he had bad news: My show wouldn't be airing on national TV. Not enough people caught onto the first five episodes, so the network was pulling the plug on the entire series. Though the news surprised me because I didn't know networks could pull shows mid-season, I wasn't upset.

I've been walking with the Lord long enough to never plan on normal. Though my show didn't air on national TV, it doesn't change the fact that I invested a great amount of money, time, energy, resources and faith into it. All the hard work that I poured into the show will not just fizzle away and disappear. The Bible is very clear that we will reap a harvest from what we sow.

I know that I sowed an obedient harvest for the Lord, so I must stay confident that all of my work will have a beautiful effect on the Kingdom of God. Although I am disappointed that I didn't get to watch my crazy adventure on TV (the episode is available online), I am really excited to see what God does with the seeds of faith that I have planted. God is always faithful, and I hold Him to His promises.

"Don't be misled—you cannot mock the justice of God. You will always harvest what you plant. Those who live only to satisfy their own sinful nature will harvest decay and death from that sinful nature. But those who live to please the Spirit will harvest everlasting life from the Spirit" (Galatians 6.7-8 NLT).

God, I know that You see all of my hard work and sacrifice, and I believe my obedience wasn't done in vain. I give my crop over to Your care because I trust that You will multiply my harvest according to Your timetable and abundance. Thank You for caring so much about my life and purpose that You take matters into Your own hands. I know that dead-ends are a part of Your plan because You are growing a generous crop in me. I pray this in Jesus' name, Amen.

Questions

1) Have you ever given God your all only to see no harvest from your efforts?

2) Do you believe that God is able to take your works of obedience and bless them in ways you could never imagine?

3) Will you claim today that the seeds you plant in obedience will produce a crop for the Lord?

Seeds of obedience will produce a harvest of blessing!

DAY 37: STORED UP MEMORIES

"But Mary treasured up all these things and pondered them in her heart" (Luke 2.19 NIV).

I have a lot of special memories stored up from my time training to be an MMA fighter for a reality TV show. One memory in particular was my initiation into my MMA training. The trainers strapped me with pads and put me in the middle of the gym mat. Then they lined up all the young MMA students (ages 4-8) in front of me. Then they gave each of them large foam sparring noodles.

The trainers explained to the young warriors that they would run to me with their sparring noodles and commence to hit me with them. I looked at the row of young kids from behind my facemask and couldn't help but laugh. They all looked so cute staring at me with gigantic, mischievous smiles and wide, excited eyes. It was obvious that they couldn't wait to attack me. One of the little faces was my son's, and I will always treasure his expression of delight.

Sometimes God asks us to do things that are difficult and uncomfortable, but those times can also provide us with our most cherished memories. I'm learning that as a Christian, life is almost never dull. God is always pushing me into crazy new areas; and I am constantly learning, growing, changing and developing. But I'm also storing up special memories in my heart, so I can pull them out to remind myself and others about our amazing God.

"The Lord is good to all; he has compassion on all he has made" (Psalm 145.9 NIV).

God, help me to trust You so completely that I'm not anxious and I don't worry, so I'll be able to appreciate the sweet moments in the middle of the storm. I don't want to rush through the difficult parts of life and miss the beauty that can only be found there. Thank You for filling my heart with priceless memories that I'll be able to reflect on the rest of my life. I pray this in Jesus' name, Amen.

Questions

1) What are some special memories of God's goodness in your life?

2) During some of your most troubling times, did God show up in amazing ways?

3) How can you look for God's love during seasons of struggle?

God will match your heartache with His grace!

DAY 38: A WARRIOR

"For our struggle is not against flesh and blood, but against the rulers, against the authorities, against the powers of this dark world and against the spiritual forces of evil in the heavenly realms" (Ephesians 6.12 NIV).

When I first met my lead trainer, he asked me if I had ever been in a fight. My answer was no. Then, he asked me why I wanted to train to be an MMA fighter. Besides following God's leading, I told him that "there is a warrior inside of me." With this single answer, I set myself up to be tested in every aspect of my life.

God was going to reveal whether or not I was truly a warrior for Him. The point was not training to be a MMA fighter; the point was finding the true warrior within me. God can use any battle we face to reveal our warrior spirits. We don't have to step inside an actual MMA cage to be warriors. There is an Enemy who is fighting us in the battlegrounds of our marriages, families, churches, schools, workplaces and minds. And His sole desire is to submit us into apathy and tap us out from our destiny.

I'm in the cage of life, and my opponent is Satan. He wants to steal my victory, but I won't let him. God has ordained Satan's eventual defeat before time began, and I need to remember that Jesus has already won the victory. I'm on the winning side, and I want to embrace the warrior God created me to be. I will not back down. I will not give up. I will not tap out. Once my fight is over, I will stand before God's throne, and my life will ring the triumphant bell of Jesus Christ!

"But thanks be to God! He gives us the victory through our Lord Jesus Christ" (1 Corinthians 15.57 NIV).

God, open my eyes so I can see my Enemy and the eternal battle raging around me. I don't want to allow my ignorance and indifference to cause me to tap out from the victory You have already declared for me. I don't want to follow the world into a conquered life that completely misses out on the glory of God. My battle is beyond the scope of this short, physical existence. I pray this in Jesus' name, Amen.

Questions

1) Did you know that Satan hates you because you are made in the image of God?

2) When you experience difficult times, how can you encourage yourself with the promises of God?

3) Is there a battle going on in your life right now that you need to claim victory?

The victory has already been won in Christ Jesus!

DAY 39: THE GLORY OF CRUSHING

"And since we are his children, we are his heirs. In fact, together with Christ we are heirs of God's glory. But if we are to share his glory, we must also share his suffering" (Romans 8.17 NLT).

I trained hard to be an MMA fighter. I had injuries upon injuries and layers of sore, sprained and hurting muscles. However, when I left the gym and went home, my pain took a backseat. When I stepped into the world of my children, I was no longer a MMA fighter—I was just mommy. My kids did not have the ability to understand and digest the depth of faith I was walking, so I did not burden them with the hardships God required me to overcome.

I gave my heartache to God and to the few people He gave to me for support. Our faith deepens through trials. Just like Job, we discover more of God's character when we find ourselves stripped of worldly comforts and standing in the middle of a storm. As we walk deeper into our crushing that triggers the awesome glory of God, we need to shield the fullness of our journey from those who will not understand it.

I know that someday I will share with my sons and daughter everything that God showed me during my time as a MMA fighter, but my stories will wait until they are ready to handle the refining process that furthers our intimacy with the Lord. For now, I'll simply be mommy to my kids—the MMA fighter can wait.

"Then the LORD spoke to Job out of the storm...." (Job 38.1 NIV).

God, I know that Your crushing is a precursor to Your glory. I have faith that once my trials are done, I will experience an abundance of Your presence from glory to glory. Remind me, though, that others will not understand the crushing that I'm experiencing; and I can't expect them to walk down this road with me. And I can't assume to fully embrace the crushing of another. I pray that You give me grace to rely solely on You when I walk by faith alone. I pray this in Jesus' name, Amen.

Questions

1) Is there a time in your life when God allowed you to experience a season of crushing?

2) Did your faith strengthen after the storm of life finally blew away?

3) How can you help others who are experiencing storms that you have already overcome?

The storm will pass, and you will stand victorious in Christ!

DAY 40: WHY JESUS?

"For God loved the world so much that he gave his one and only Son, so that everyone who believes in him will not perish but have eternal life" (John 3.16 NLT).

One of the producers from the reality show was driving me to our next location, so I had a full ten minutes of her undivided attention. I asked her if I could give her my spiel about why I believe in Jesus. She shrugged and gave me the go-ahead, and I dove right into what the Holy Spirit had taught me.

God created a perfect world with a perfect people; however, He gave us free will. Free will is a gift and a burden. It is a gift because it allows us to create good (inside of God), but it is a burden because we can choose to create evil (outside of God). Everything that exists has its absence. God didn't create evil; but because God exists, the absence of God (evil) exists. Our free will separates us from our perfect God because we are no longer perfect.

God knew we would use our free will to sin, so He also created a Redemption Plan. He left His glory and sent Himself into this world in the form of a man named Jesus over two thousand years ago. Jesus lived a perfect life and died on the cross for our sins. By faith we wear Jesus' perfection, and by grace He took our imperfection. If we accept His sacrifice for our sins, we stand righteous before a perfect God.

The Holy Spirit becomes our guide and the Bible becomes our map to achieving the purposes God created for us before time began. Once our bodies die, we can stand before God in eternity (heaven) because we are clothed in the righteousness of Jesus; and we will be rewarded for living a life of faith for Him. The gift of salvation is ours if we only ask, but a relationship with God is only possible through Jesus.

"Jesus told him, 'I am the way, the truth, and the life. No one can come to the Father except through me'" (John 14.6 NLT).

God, when I die, I want to be able to live with You in heaven. As hard as I try, I will never be perfect enough to get to heaven by myself. I pray that You cover me with the righteousness of Jesus. I trust that He died for my sins, and I freely ask for forgiveness. Please give me the Holy Spirit. Unlock the power of the Bible when I read it, so I can apply its Truth to my life. I pray this by faith in Jesus' name. Amen.

Questions

1) Have you accepted Jesus Christ as your Lord and Savior?

2) Did you know that Jesus' finished work on the cross has redeemed your relationship with God?

3) How can you enjoy your relationship with God today, knowing that your sins are forgiven?

Jesus is the only way to God!

Thank you for following me on this Mixed Martial Arts journey. I hope you enjoyed this devotional book. May you be filled with the love of our Creator, the wisdom of our Counselor and the courage of our Savior.

If you would like to read any of my other books, check out my Amazon Page. You can find me at alisahopewagner.com, Facebook, Twitter, YouTube, Instagram and Goodreads. My social media handle is @alisahopewagner.

If you enjoyed this book, I would very much appreciate a review on **Amazon**. Scroll under the reviews and click "Write a Customer Review." Give your stars and a few words of encouragement!